First Facts

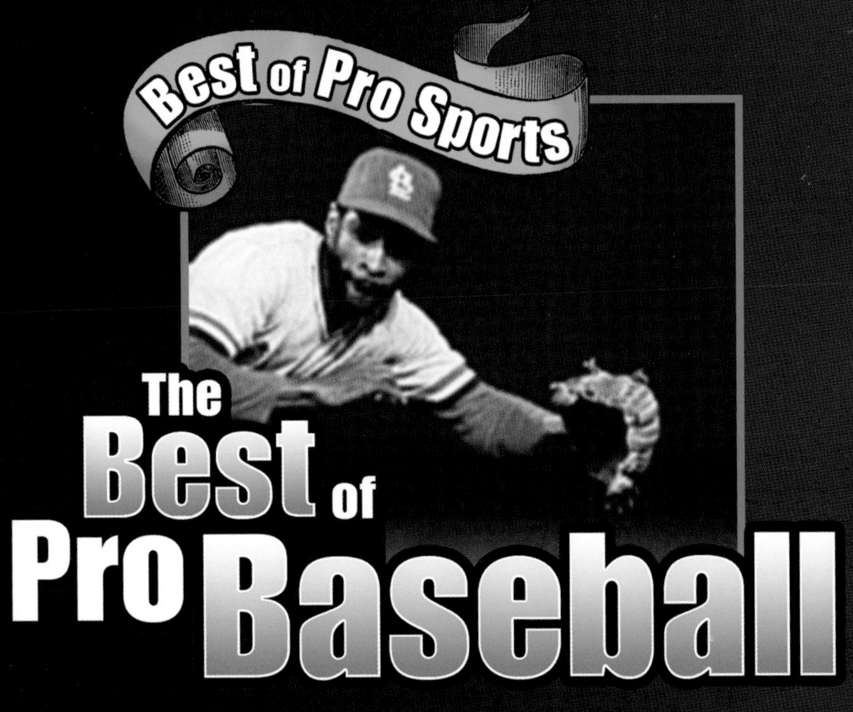

The Best of Pro Baseball

by Matt Doeden

Consultant:
Craig R. Coenen, PhD
Associate Professor of History
Mercer County Community College
West Windsor, New Jersey

Capstone press
Mankato, Minnesota

First Facts is published by Capstone Press,
151 Good Counsel Drive, P.O. Box 669, Mankato, Minnesota 56002.
www.capstonepress.com

Printed in the United States of America

Books published by Capstone Press are manufactured with paper containing at least 10 percent post-consumer waste.

Library of Congress Cataloging-in-Publication Data
Doeden, Matt.
The best of pro baseball / by Matt Doeden.
p. cm. — (First facts. Best of pro sports)
Includes bibliographical references and index.
Summary: "Presents some of the best moments and players in professional baseball history" — Provided by publisher.
ISBN 978-1-4296-3329-1 (library binding)
ISBN 978-1-4296-3876-0 (softcover)
1. Baseball — United States — History — Juvenile literature. I. Title. II. Series.
GV867.5.D64 2010
796.357'640973 — dc22 2009001168

Editorial Credits
Christopher Harbo, editor; Kyle Grenz, designer; Eric Gohl, media researcher

Photo Credits
AP Images, 5, 11; Amy Sancetta, 13 (left); Charles Krupa, cover; Harry Harris, 9 (bottom)
Corbis/Bettmann, 14–15
Getty Images Inc./AFP/David Maxwell, 13 (right); AFP/Matt Campbell, 17 (bottom); Focus On Sport, 7 (left); MLB Photos/Ron Vesely, 18; Sports Imagery/Ronald C. Modra, 1, 17 (top), 20–21; Transcendental Graphics/Mark Rucker, 9 (top)
Library of Congress, 7 (right)
Shutterstock/Adrian Coroama, baseball; Kenneth Sponsler, baseball field background; Pertusinas, tickets

Essential content terms are **bold** and are defined at the bottom of the spread where they first appear.

Table of Contents

Best Catch 4
Best Pitcher 6
Best Home Run 8
Best Slugger 10
Best Comeback 12
Best Pitching Performance 14
Best Base-Stealer 16
Best World Series 19
Best Fielder 20

Glossary 22
Read More 23
Internet Sites 23
Index 24

Best Catch

No player has matched "The Catch" by Willie Mays. He made it in game one of the 1954 World Series. The New York Giants and the Cleveland Indians were tied. Two runners were on base. The Indians' Vic Wertz then drove the ball deep to center field. Mays sprinted toward the wall. He made the amazing catch over his left shoulder.

Best Pitcher

The Dodgers' Sandy Koufax pitched for just 12 seasons. But starting in 1961, he put together baseball's greatest stretch of pitching. Over six years, he won 129 games and struck out 1,713 hitters. He had four **no-hitters**. He also won three Cy Young Awards.

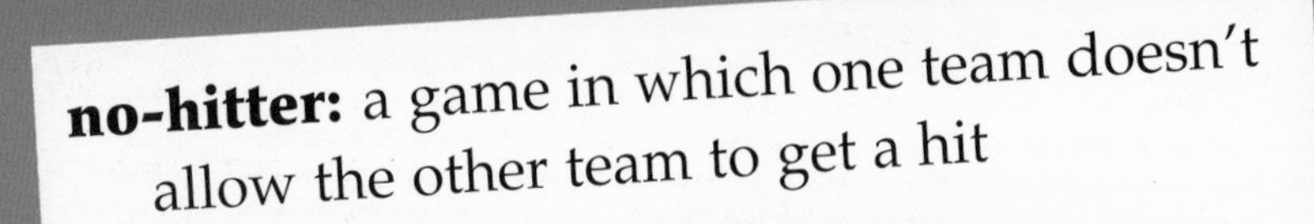

no-hitter: a game in which one team doesn't allow the other team to get a hit

Runner-up

Cy Young won 511 games from 1890 to 1911. That's more wins than any pitcher in history. Young died in 1955. One year later, baseball began honoring him. Each year, the best pitcher in each league receives the Cy Young Award.

Best Home Run

In a 1951 playoff game, the Brooklyn Dodgers led the New York Giants. There was one out in the bottom of the ninth inning. Bobby Thomson stepped up to bat for the Giants. He **slugged** a three-run homer over the left-field wall. It won the game. The home run is known as "The Shot Heard 'Round the World."

slug: to hit with force

Is It a Tie?

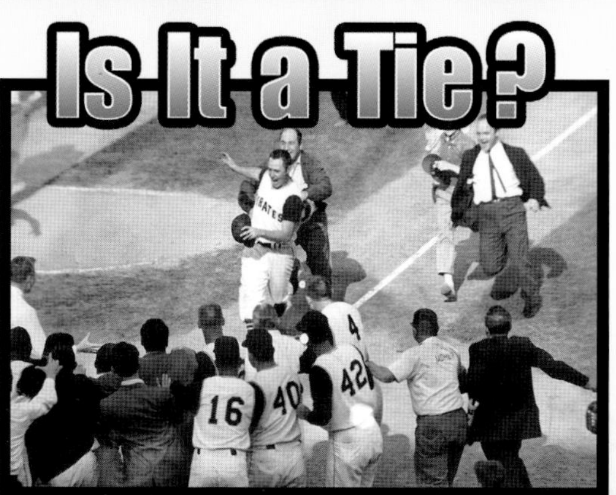

Bill Mazeroski ended the 1960 World Series with a home run. His solo shot broke a 9-9 tie to win game seven for Pittsburgh. Was Mazeroski's homer the best in baseball history?

Best Slugger

Who's the greatest slugger in baseball history? Names like Barry Bonds, Hank Aaron, and Alex Rodriguez come to mind. But Babe Ruth stands above them all. Ruth hit 714 career home runs at a time when they were rare. No other slugger can compare.

Slugging Percentage

A batter's slugging percentage measures power hitting and batting average. Babe Ruth's career slugging percentage record is .690. This record has stood for more than 70 years.

Best Comeback

It was the 2004 playoffs. The Boston Red Sox trailed the New York Yankees three games to none. No team had ever blown a 3-0 playoff series lead. But in the 12th inning of game four, David Ortiz blasted a home run. This shot gave the Sox a win. Ortiz's home run lit a fire under his team. Boston came back to win the playoff series.

Runner-up

One of the best single-game comebacks came on August 5, 2001. The Cleveland Indians trailed the Seattle Mariners 12-0 after three innings. But the Indians fought back. They won 15-14 in 11 innings.

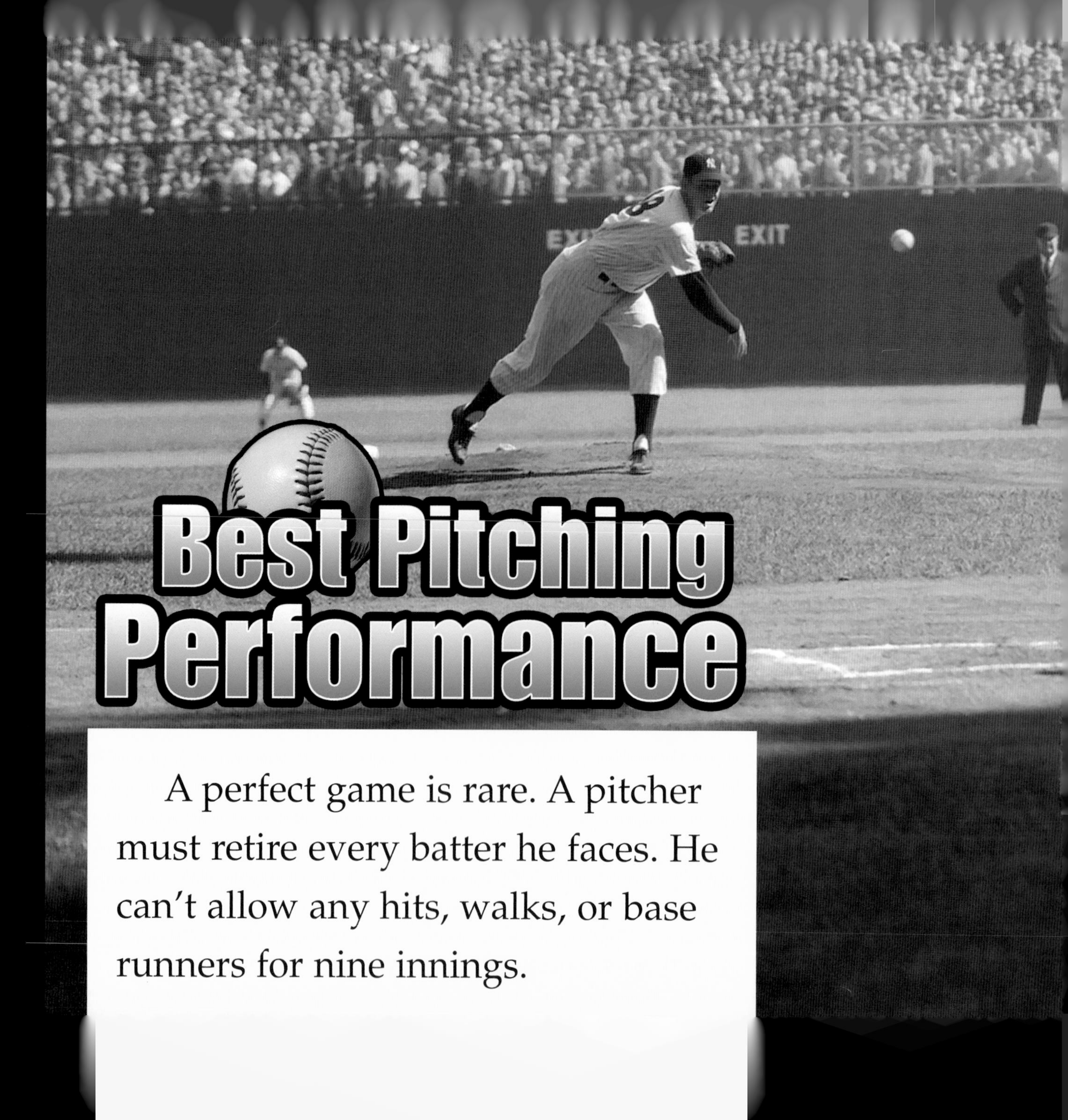

Best Pitching Performance

A perfect game is rare. A pitcher must retire every batter he faces. He can't allow any hits, walks, or base runners for nine innings.

New York Yankee pitcher Don Larsen was perfect in the 1956 World Series. His perfect game helped the Yankees win the World Series.

Best Base-Stealer

Nobody ran the bases like Rickey Henderson. The speedy outfielder stole 1,406 bases in his career. That's almost 500 more than second-place Lou Brock. Henderson led the league in steals 12 times. In 1982, he shattered Brock's single-season record with 130 steals. What a thief!

Most Runs Scored

Rickey Henderson is also baseball's all-time leader in runs scored. He crossed the plate 2,295 times.

Twins
34

Best World Series

The 1991 World Series was full of **drama**. Three games between the Minnesota Twins and the Atlanta Braves went extra innings. Four games were decided on the last pitch. The Twins' Kirby Puckett won game six with an extra-inning home run. In game seven, Minnesota's Jack Morris pitched 10 shutout innings for a 1-0 victory. Talk about a nail-biter!

drama: exciting or intense events

Best Fielder

shortstop: the defensive position between second and third base

To many baseball fans, the Wizard of Oz was the game's greatest fielder. Ozzie Smith was an amazing **shortstop**. He made hard plays look easy. When a baseball took a bad bounce, he didn't need a glove. A bare hand was enough for the Wiz.

drama (DRAH-muh) — exciting or intense events

league (LEEG) — a group of sports teams; professional baseball is made up of the National League and the American League.

no-hitter (no-HIT-ur) — a game in which one team doesn't allow the other team to get a hit

retire (ri-TIRE) — to put out in baseball

shortstop (SHORT-stop) — in baseball or softball, the defensive position between second and third base

slug (SLUG) — to hit with force

Read More

Christopher, Matt. *The World Series: Great Championship Moments.* Legendary Sports Events. New York: Little, Brown and Company, 2007.

Doeden, Matt. *The Greatest Baseball Records.* Sports Records. Mankato, Minn.: Capstone Press, 2009.

Wong, Stephen. *Baseball Treasures.* New York: Smithsonian, 2007.

Internet Sites

FactHound offers a safe, fun way to find Internet sites related to this book. All of the sites on FactHound have been researched by our staff.

Here's all you do:

Visit *www.facthound.com*

FactHound will fetch the best sites for you!

Index

Brock, Lou, 16

catches, 4
comebacks, 12, 13
Cy Young Awards, 6, 7

fielders, 16, 21

Henderson, Rickey, 16, 17
home runs, 8, 9, 10, 12, 19

Koufax, Sandy, 6

Larsen, Don, 15

Mays, Willie, 4
Mazeroski, Bill, 9
Morris, Jack, 19

no-hitters, 6

Ortiz, David, 12

perfect games, 14–15
pitchers, 6, 7, 14–15
playoffs, 4, 8, 9, 12, 15, 19
Puckett, Kirby, 19

Ruth, Babe, 10, 11

slugging percentage, 11
Smith, Ozzie, 21
stolen bases, 16

Thomson, Bobby, 8

Wertz, Vic, 4
World Series, 4, 9, 15, 19

Young, Cy, 7